LIFE IN THE — U.S. — MARINE CORPS

by Mari Bolte

PEBBLE
a capstone imprint

Published by Pebble, an imprint of Capstone
1710 Roe Crest Drive, North Mankato, Minnesota 56003
capstonepub.com

Copyright © 2025 by Capstone. All rights reserved. No part of this publication may be reproduced in whole or in part, or stored in a retrieval system, or transmitted in any form or by any means, electronic, mechanical, photocopying, recording, or otherwise, without written permission of the publisher.

Library of Congress Cataloging-in-Publication Data is available on the Library of Congress website.

ISBN: 9780756579913 (hardcover)
ISBN: 9780756580186 (paperback)
ISBN: 9780756579975 (ebook PDF)

Summary: Gives readers a peek into daily life for U.S. Marines.

Editorial Credits
Editor: Mandy Robbins; Designer: Heidi Thompson; Media Researcher: Jo Miller; Production Specialist: Tori Abraham

Image Credits
Shutterstock/Pamela Au, 19, Picksell, background (throughout), Sergey Novikov, 21; U.S. Marine Corps photo by Cpl. Jamin M. Powell, 5, Cpl. Luke Kuennen, Cover (top right), Cpl. Nicole Lavine, Cover (top left), Cpl. Samuel A. Nasso, 17, Cpl. Samuel Guerra, 15, Cpl. Travis Gershaneck, 9, Lance Cpl. Aaron S. Patterson, MCBH Combat Camera, 14, Lance Cpl. Brandon Maldonado, Cover (bottom), Lance Cpl. Charles Santamaria, 8, Lance Cpl. Chelsea Anderson, 18, Lance Cpl. Isaiah Gomez, 7, Lance Cpl. Jodson B. Graves, 12, Lance Cpl. Joshua McAlpine, 11, Lance Cpl. Samantha Draughon, Cover (top middle), Lance Cpl. Hernan Vidana, MCIPAC Combat Camera, 10, Sgt. Aaron Henson, 13, Staff Sgt. Dengrier M. Baez, 16

The appearance of U.S. Department of Defense (DoD) visual information does not imply or constitute DoD endorsement.

Any additional websites and resources referenced in this book are not maintained, authorized, or sponsored by Capstone. All product and company names are trademarks™ or registered® trademarks of their respective holders.

Printed in the United States   6340

TABLE OF CONTENTS

Boots on the Ground 4

Life on Base 6

Marine Routine 10

Deployments 14

Marine Strong 20

    Glossary 22

    Read More 23

    Internet Sites 23

    Index 24

    About the Author 24

Words in **bold** appear in the glossary.

BOOTS ON THE GROUND

Members of the United States Marine Corps leap into action whenever there is a **crisis**. They can be found around the world.

Marines have many jobs. Each one is important. Marines fly planes and helicopters. Others drive armored vehicles. They serve on ships. They protect **bases**.

Marines do a training exercise.

LIFE ON BASE

Many Marines live on bases. Bases are towns for members of the military. There are places to shop and eat together. Doctors at clinics keep Marines feeling their best.

Marines may be far away from friends and family members. Bases help Marines feel at home.

A store at Camp Lejeune, a military base

Not everyone on a base is a Marine. Military **spouses** may have jobs on base. Kids go to school there.

Many bases have special activities for those who live there. Families can play golf or swim. Hiking and biking trails help them stay active. Near some bases, people can ski or even hunt!

MARINE ROUTINE

Marines are problem solvers. They set goals. Then they ask questions. Is the goal realistic? How long will it take? What steps are needed? Marines make daily routines to reach their goals. Daily routines mean **discipline**.

Marines must have strong bodies and minds. No matter what their job, each Marine must pass two tests every six months. One is called the Physical Fitness Test. The other is the Combat Fitness Test. These two tests help keep Marines ready for action.

DEPLOYMENTS

Marines show up whenever there is a crisis. They might be called in at any time. And they must be ready for **deployment** right away!

Marines protect important leaders. They work with other military branches. If there is a **natural disaster**, they show up to help out. If there is a war, Marines will be there to fight.

Deployments can last from six months to more than a year. Many Marines serve aboard Navy ships. Others take planes around the world. For every six months that a Marine is deployed, they are home for about a year.

Marines usually serve between four and six years. Some then join the Marine Corps **Reserve**. This group of part-time Marines are ready to help out if the Marine Corps need backup.

Others join the Marine Corps League. They keep up traditions and support active service members. "Once a Marine, always a Marine" is their official **motto**.

MARINE STRONG

Test your fitness like a Marine. Grab a stopwatch or a friend to help count. Then, give it your all!

How many pull-ups can you do? How many push-ups can you do? Can you run three miles? What was your time? How long can you hold a plank?

GLOSSARY

base (BAYS)—an area run by the military where people serving in the military live and military supplies are stored

crisis (KRYE-siss)—a time of danger or difficulty

deployment (di-PLOY-ment)—when troops move to a particular location to prepare for military action

discipline (DIS-uh-plin)—self-control and the ability to follow the rules

motto (MOTT-oh)—words that tell what someone believes in or stands for

natural disaster (NACH-ur-uhl di-ZAS-tuhr)—a flood, storm, earthquake, or other deadly event caused by nature

reserves (ri-ZURVZ)—troops that stay ready for active duty but are not full-time soldiers

spouse (SPOWSS)—a person's legal life partner

READ MORE

Gish, Ashley. *Marine Force Recon*. Mankato, MN: Creative Education, 2022.

London, Martha. *US Marine Corps Equipment and Vehicles*. Minneapolis: Kids Core, an imprint of Abdo Publishing, 2022.

Pallotta, Jerry, and Sammie Garnett. *U.S. Marines Alphabet Book*. Watertown, MA: Charlesbridge, 2021.

INTERNET SITES

Britannica Kids: Marines
kids.britannica.com/kids/article/marines/353430

Life in the Marine Corps
marines.com/life-as-a-marine/life-in-the-marine-corps.html

Ready Marine Corps Kids
www.ready.marines.mil/Ready-Marine-Corps-Kids/

INDEX

bases, 4, 6, 7, 8, 9

deployments, 14, 16

fitness tests, 12, 20

goals, 10

jobs, 4, 6, 8, 12

Marine Corps League, 19
Marine Corps Reserve, 18
motto, 19

natural disasters, 15

planes, 4, 16

routines, 10

ships, 4, 16

training, 5

war, 15

ABOUT THE AUTHOR

Mari Bolte is the author and editor of hundreds of children's books. Every book is her favorite book as long as the readers learned something and enjoyed themselves!